50 FRENCH PHRASES

Catherine Bruzzone & Susan Martineau

French adviser: Marie-Thérèse Bougard

Illustrations by Leighton Noyes

Contents

Special note for learners!

The key French phrases you will learn are numbered on each spread. There are also extra words you will need for the activities. By the end of the book you will know 50 FRENCH PHRASES and lots of useful French words. There is a summary of all these at the back of the book.

Listen to the audio on our website!

Scan the QR code on the back cover of this book with the camera app on your smartphone or tablet. Contact us on books@bsmall.co.uk if you need any support with this.

If you cannot access this, the simple pronunciation guide in the book will help. Read the words as naturally as possible, as if they were English.

Bonjour!

Have some fun saying hello and goodbye in French. You need to match the right greeting to the pictures, according to the time of day illustrated. Say the correct phrase out loud. You can check your answers on page 32.

1

Bonjour
boh-shoor
Hello, good morning

2

Au revoir
oh r'vwahr
Goodbye

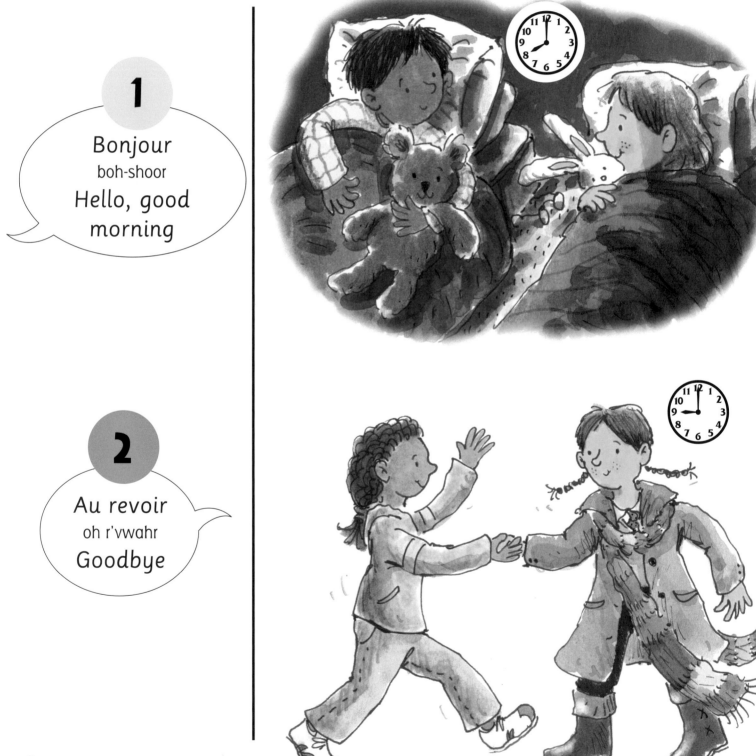

3

Bonsoir
boh-swahr
Good evening

4

Bonne nuit
bon nwee
Goodnight

Words to Know

Salut!	à bientôt	le jour	le soir	la nuit
saloo	ah bee-an-toh	ler shoor	ler swahr	la nwee
Hi!	See you soon	day	evening	night

Je m'appelle...

Ask your friends or family to play this naming game with you. One person needs to be blindfolded and twirled round. They then have to 'find' someone and ask **Comment tu t'appelles?** The person answers **Je m'appelle...** and says **Et toi?** Take it in turns to be the 'finder'. You could all choose a French name!

5

Comment tu t'appelles?
kom-oh too tapell
What's your name?

6

Je m'appelle...
sh' mapell...
My name is...

Choose a Name

Alexandre
alex-ahn-dr

Antoine
ahn-twahn

Marie
ma-ree

Sarah
sah-rah

Nicolas
nee-kol-ah

Thomas
toe-mah

Camille
kam-eel

Manon
ma-noh

Quel âge as-tu?

You will need two dice for this game. One person throws them and the other asks **Quel âge as-tu?** The dice thrower answers **J'ai... ans**, putting in the number the dice add up to.
Take it in turns.

8

Quel âge as-tu?
kell ah-sh ah-too
How old are you?

9

J'ai neuf ans
shay nerf ahn
I am nine years old

10

Bon anniversaire!
bon-anni-vairsair
Happy birthday!

Numbers! Numbers!

1	**un**	ahn		7	**sept**	set
2	**deux**	der		8	**huit**	weet
3	**trois**	trwah		9	**neuf**	nerf
4	**quatre**	katr'		10	**dix**	deess
5	**cinq**	sank		11	**onze**	onz
6	**six**	seess		12	**douze**	dooz

Look at the numbers on the inside front cover if you want to ask some older people their ages!

Ça va?

Cut out a circle of paper or card. Draw a smiley face on one side and a sad one on the other. Ask a friend **Ça va?** as you show them one of the faces. They have to try and give the right answer depending on if it is smiley or glum. Swap round so that you can practise too.

11

Ça va?
sa-vah
How are you?

12

Ça va bien, merci
sa-vah bee-ah mair-see
I'm fine, thanks

13

Ça ne va pas bien
sa ner vah pah bee-ah
I'm not so well

Words to Know

affreux
ah-frer
awful

assez bien
ah-seh bee-ah
quite well

comme ci
comme ça
kom see kom sa
so-so

très bien
treh bee-ah
very good

merci
mair-see
thank you

Où est...?

Find all of the items in the **Words to Know** list and put them on a tray. Practise saying the French words for them. Now close your eyes while a friend takes one item off the tray. (Cover up the French words too.) You then have to ask **Où est le/la...?** whatever the missing thing is! Your friend will either say **Voilà le/la...** or **Encore une fois!** Take it in turns to have a go at remembering.

14

Où est...?
oo eh
Where is...?

15

Voilà le/la...
vwah-lah ler/lah
Here is the...

16

Encore une fois!
on-kor yoon fwah
Try again!

A note about le and la

There are two words for 'the' in French – **le** and **la**. Try to learn them when you learn a new noun.

Words to Know

le livre	**le papier**	**le crayon de couleur**	**la gomme**
ler leevr'	ler papee-eh	ler cray-oh der cool-err	lah gom
book	paper	colour pencil	rubber
le crayon	**le stylo**	**la colle**	**la règle**
ler cray-oh	ler steelo	lah koll	lah ray-gl'
pencil	pen	glue	ruler

Qu'est-ce que c'est?

Look at this outdoor scene and practise saying the French words.
Then ask some friends or your family to play a drawing game with
you. You each take it in turns to draw one of the named items and
ask **Qu'est-ce-que c'est?** Everyone else has to try and say what it is
from the drawing (and without looking at the French words).
They say **C'est un/une....**

17

Qu'est-ce que
c'est?

kesker seh

What is it?

une fille
oon fee
girl

un vélo
ahn vaylo
bicycle

12

un oiseau
ahn nwas-o
bird

un ballon
ahn balloh
ball

18

C'est un/une...
set ahn/oon
It's a...

un sac à dos
ahn sak ah doh
backpack

un banc
ahn boh
bench

un pique-nique
ahn peek-neek
picnic

un garçon
ahn gar-soh
boy

A note about un and une
There are two words for 'a' in French – **un**
and **une**. You say **C'est un** for a **le** word and
C'est une for a **la** word. For example, **C'est une**
fille or **C'est un banc**.

13

Voici la famille

Spot the family! Look at page 15. Which four people are members of the same family? Point them out and say **Voici le fils** or **Voici la fille**. Use other words from **Words to Know** with **Voici** too. When you have found the whole family, you can say **Voici la famille**.
Check your answers on page 32.

19
Voici le fils
vwah-see ler fees
Here's the son

20
Voici la fille
vwah-see lah fee
Here's the daughter

21
Voici la famille
vwah-see lah fam-ee
Here's the family

Words to Know

la mère/maman
lah mair/mamoh
mother/mum

le père/papa
ler pair/papa
father/dad

les parents
leh pah-roh
parents

la sœur
lah sir
sister

le frère
ler frair
brother

le bébé
ler beh-beh
baby

la grand-mère
lah groh-mair
grandmother

le grand-père
ler groh-pair
grandfather

J'aime...

Have a look at this picture and try to learn the French words for everything. Then choose four things you like and four you don't like. Practise saying if you like them or not by using the phrases **J'aime...** and **Je n'aime pas....** For example, **J'aime les fleurs** or **Je n'aime pas les moustiques**. Practise with a friend and take turns.

les moustiques
lay mooss-teek
mosquitos

22

J'aime...
shem
I like...

23

Je n'aime pas...
sh'nem pah
I don't like...

les chèvres
lay shevr
goats

les lapins
lay lah-pah
rabbits

les fleurs
lay fler
flowers

les chats
lay shah
cats

le soleil
ler solay
sun

la pluie
lah ploo-ee
rain

les arbres
lay zar-br'
trees

les canards
lay can-ar
ducks

les cochons
lay koh-shoh
pigs

les chiens
lay shee-yah
dogs

les araignées
lay zaray-nee-ay
spiders

Où habites-tu?

The children in the pictures are telling us where they live. Practise saying the phrases. Then cut out four pieces of paper to cover speech bubbles 25-28 and number them from 1 to 4. Ask a friend or adult to call out **un**, **deux**, **trois** or **quatre** and say **Où habites-tu?** You have to try and remember how to say where you live according to the scene next to the number.

24

Où habites-tu?
oo ab-eet too
Where do you live?

25

J'habite une maison
sh'ab-eet oon meh-zoh
I live in a house

26

J'habite un appartement
sh'ab-eet ahn appa-ter-moh
I live in an apartment

Je voudrais...

Have some fun with this French shopping game for two or more people. Look at the shopping list and practise the words. The first player says **Je voudrais des pommes, s'il vous plaît** and then points at the next thing on the list, the strawberries, on the market stall. The next player has to add them to the phrase, saying **Je voudrais des pommes et des fraises, s'il vous plaît**. Each player adds another thing to the list. The winner is the first one to say the whole list correctly. Then you can shout **C'est tout, merci**.

29

Je voudrais...
sh' vood-reh
I would like...

30

S'il vous plaît
seel-voo-pleh
Please

31

C'est tout, merci
seh too mair-see
That's all, thanks

The Shopping List

des pommes
deh pom
(some) apples

des fraises
deh fraiz
(some) strawberries

des bananes
deh ban-an
(some) bananas

des raisins
deh ray-zah
(some) grapes

des carottes
deh kah-rot
(some) carrots

des pommes de terre
deh pom der tair
(some) potatoes

des tomates
deh tom-at
(some) tomatoes

de la salade
der lah sah-lad
(some) salad/lettuce

Un verre d'eau, s'il vous plaît

It's time to eat so have a go at asking for food and drink in French. You can ask a friend or adult to say **Qu'est-ce que tu veux?** All you need to do is choose something tasty from the menu and add **s'il vous plaît**. You might also like to say **J'ai faim** or **J'ai soif**.

**Un verre d'eau,
s'il vous plaît**
ahn vair doh seel-voo-pleh
A glass of water,
please

Menu/Le menu ler men-yoo

un jus d'orange
ahn joo dor-ronsh
an orange juice

un verre d'eau
ahn vair doh
a glass of water

un verre de lait
ahn vair der lay
a glass of milk

un morceau de gâteau
ahn morso der gat-o
a piece of cake

des chips
deh sheep
some crisps

des fruits
deh froo-ee
some fruit

du pain
dew pan
some bread

du jambon
dew shomboh
some ham

du fromage
dew fromah-sh
some cheese

un yaourt
ahn yah-oort
a yogurt

Qu'est-ce que tu veux faire?

You need two or more people to play this acting game. Read the phrases and then cover them up. One of you asks **Qu'est-ce que tu veux faire?** and acts out one of the activities. The other player, or players, answer **Je veux...** whatever they think the activity is. Take it in turns to be the actor.

36

Qu'est-ce que tu veux faire?
kesker too ver fair
What do you want to do?

37

Je veux regarder la télé
sh' ver r'gar-deh lah teh-leh
I want to watch TV

38

Je veux jouer au football
sh' ver shoo-eh oh footbol
I want to play football

39

Je veux faire du vélo
sh' ver fair doo vaylo
I want to cycle

40

Je veux nager
sh' ver nah-shay
I want to go swimming

Words to Know

Tu veux...?
too ver
Do you want to...?

Oui, je veux bien
wee sh' ver bee-ah
Yes, I'd like to

Non, merci
noh mair-see
No thanks

C'est de quelle couleur?

Here's a fun game to help you practise colours in French with your friends or family. You will need a die and some counters. When you land on a square all the other players shout **C'est de quelle couleur?** You say **Ma couleur préférée, c'est le rouge** or whatever colour you have landed on. If you get the answer wrong you miss a turn. Good luck!

41

C'est de quelle couleur?
seh de kel koo-ler
What colour is it?

START

FINISH

42

Quelle est ta couleur préférée?
kel eh tah koo-ler prayfeh-reh
What's your favourite colour?

Count in French as you move your counter.

43

Ma couleur préférée, c'est le...
mah koo-ler prayfeh-reh seh ler...
My favourite colour is...

Colours/Les couleurs leh koo-ler

rouge	**vert**	**noir**	**orange**
rooshj	vair	nwah	oranshj
red	green	black	orange
bleu	**jaune**	**blanc**	**marron**
bl'	shown	bloh	mah-roh
blue	yellow	white	brown

Où vas-tu?

These children are all dressed for their holidays. See if you can match the right phrases to the children. Say **Où vas-tu?** and then choose the right answering phrase. Practise saying this out loud too.
Check your answers on page 32.

44

Où vas-tu?
oo vah too
Where are you going?

45

Je vais à la plage
sh' vey ah lah plah-sh
I'm going to the beach

46

Je vais à la campagne
sh' vey ah lah kom-pine-y'
I'm going to the country

47

Je vais à la montagne
sh' vey ah lah mon-tine-y'
I'm going to the mountains

48

Je vais en ville
sh' vey ahn veel
I'm going to town

Words to Know

en vacances
ahn vak-onss
on holiday

Bon voyage!
boh vwoy-ah-sh
Have a good
journey!

Je porte...

It is time to get dressed – in French! Have a look at the first picture and say **Je porte un petit pantalon**. Now look at the second picture and describe the difference in the trousers. Say **Je porte un grand pantalon**. Carry on describing the differences between the clothes on page 31. You'll need to use the **Words to Know** and have a look at the note about how to say 'big' and 'small' in French. You can check the answers on page 32.

49

Je porte un petit pantalon
sh' port ahn p'tee pantah-loh
I'm wearing small trousers

50

Je porte un grand pantalon
sh' port ahn groh pantah-loh
I'm wearing big trousers

Big or small?

If the noun you are describing is a **le (un)** word, you use **grand** or **petit**. If the noun is a **la (une)** word, you use **grande** or **petite**. For example, **un grand manteau** or **une grande robe**; **un petit manteau** or **une petite robe**.

Words to Know

un pantalon
ahn pantah-loh
trousers

un manteau
ahn man-to
a coat

un tee-shirt
ahn tee-shairt
a T-shirt

une casquette
oon kasket
a cap

une jupe
oon shoop
a skirt

un sweat
ahn sweet
a sweatshirt

petit/petite
p'tee/p'-teet
small

grand/grande
groh/grond
big

31

Solutions/Answers

Here are the answers to the activities on pages 2-3, 14-15, 28-29 and 30-31.

pages 2-3

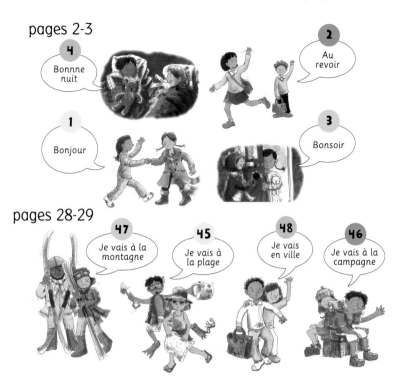

4 Bonne nuit
2 Au revoir
1 Bonjour
3 Bonsoir

pages 14-15

Voici la mère/maman

Voici le grand-père

Voici la fille/la sœur

Voici le fils/le frère

pages 28-29

47 Je vais à la montagne
45 Je vais à la plage
48 Je vais en ville
46 Je vais à la campagne

pages 30-31

Je porte un grand manteau   Je porte un petit manteau

Je porte un grand tee-shirt   Je porte un petit tee-shirt

Je porte une grande jupe   Je porte une petite jupe

Je porte un grand sweat   Je porte un petit sweat

Je porte une grande casquette   Je porte une petite casquette

50 phrases français/50 French Phrases

1 **Bonjour** Hello, good morning
2 **Au revoir** Goodbye
3 **Bonsoir** Good evening
4 **Bonne nuit** Goodnight
5 **Comment tu t'appelles?** What's your name?
6 **Je m'appelle…** My name is…
7 **Et toi?** And you?
8 **Quel âge as-tu?** How old are you?
9 **J'ai neuf ans** I am nine years old
10 **Bon anniversaire!** Happy birthday!
11 **Ça va?** How are you?
12 **Ça va bien, merci** I'm fine, thanks
13 **Ça ne va pas bien** I'm not so well
14 **Où est…?** Where is…?
15 **Voilà le/la…** Here is the…
16 **Encore une fois!** Try again!
17 **Qu'est-ce que c'est?** What is it?
18 **C'est un/une…** It's a…
19 **Voici le fils** Here's the son
20 **Voici la fille** Here's the daughter
21 **Voici la famille** Here's the family
22 **J'aime…** I like…
23 **Je n'aime pas…** I don't like…
24 **Où habites-tu?** Where do you live?
25 **J'habite une maison** I live in a house
26 **J'habite un appartement** I live in an apartment
27 **J'habite en ville** I live in town
28 **J'habite à la campagne** I live in the country
29 **Je voudrais…** I would like…
30 **S'il vous plaît** Please
31 **C'est tout, merci** That's all, thanks
32 **Qu'est-ce que tu veux?** What would you like?
33 **J'ai faim** I'm hungry
34 **J'ai soif** I'm thirsty
35 **Un verre d'eau, s'il vous plaît** A glass of water, please
36 **Qu'est-ce que tu veux faire?** What do you want to do?
37 **Je veux regarder la télé** I want to watch TV
38 **Je veux jouer au football** I want to play football
39 **Je veux faire du vélo** I want to cycle
40 **Je veux nager** I want to go swimming
41 **C'est de quelle couleur?** What colour is it?
42 **Quelle est ta couleur préférée?** What's your favourite colour?
43 **Ma couleur préférée, c'est le…** My favourite colour is…
44 **Où vas-tu?** Where are you going?
45 **Je vais à la plage** I'm going to the beach
46 **Je vais à la campagne** I'm going to the country
47 **Je vais à la montagne** I'm going to the mountains
48 **Je vais en ville** I'm going to town
49 **Je porte un petit pantalon** I'm wearing small trousers
50 **Je porte un grand pantalon** I'm wearing big trousers